Progress with Oxford

W0051260

Age 4-5

Starting to Write Letters

Hello! I'm Penn. This is Sill.

Contents

Key

 Circle

 Match

 Draw

 Write

 Trace with finger

 Trace with pencil

 Play together

 Find the sticker

 Colour

OXFORD
UNIVERSITY PRESS

Pencil grip

 Pick up your pencil and hold it like this.

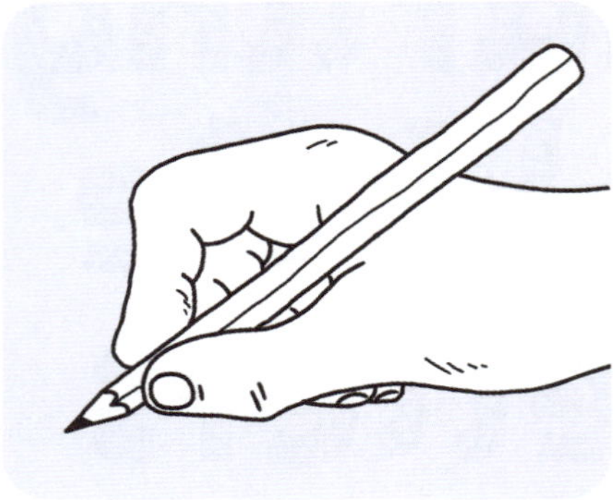

Right hand

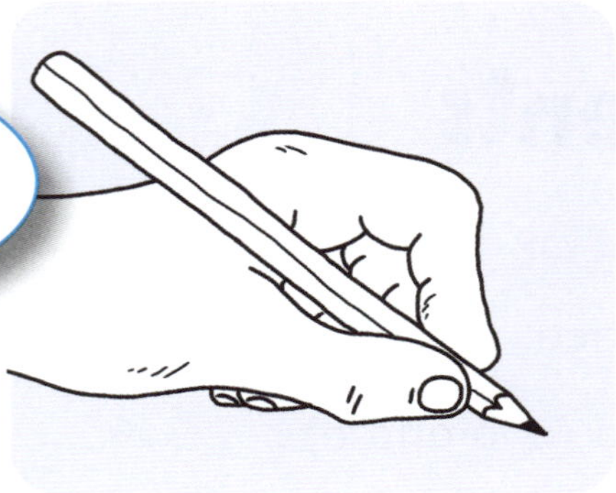

Left hand

Pick up your pencil!

Trace the patterns.

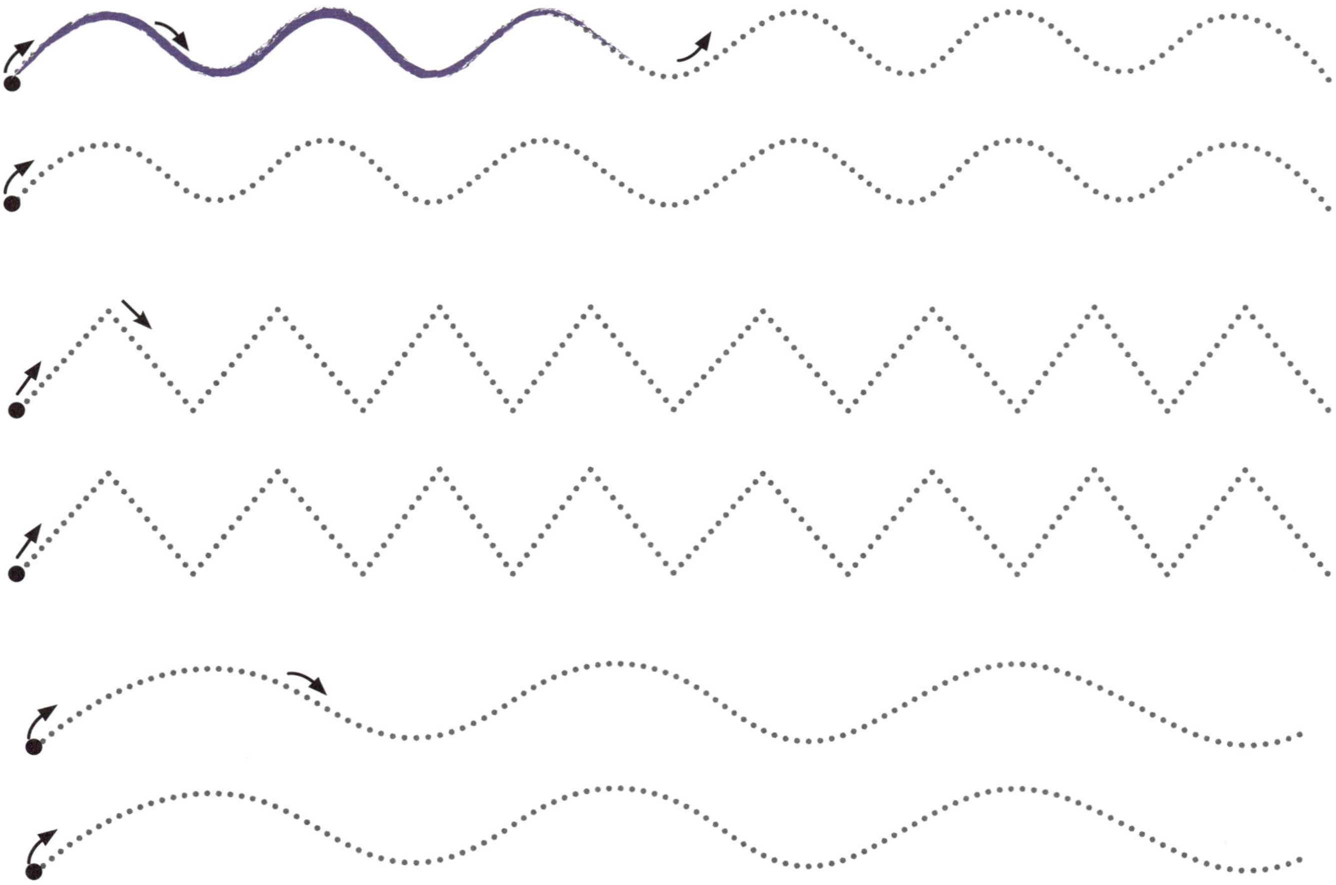

Trace the patterns.

Keep practising with your pencil.

Exercise your hands and fingers!

Well done!

Play with your hands.

Take a lump of dough in each hand. Squeeze the dough in time to your favourite song.

Practise picking up very small things. Sort out a button box or sort beads into different colours.

Thread breakfast hoops or pasta tubes on to a chopstick or uncooked spaghetti. Thread big beads on to string.

Give yourself a sticker

Now – track how you're doing on page 32!

Pencil practice

 Trace the patterns.

 Round and round!

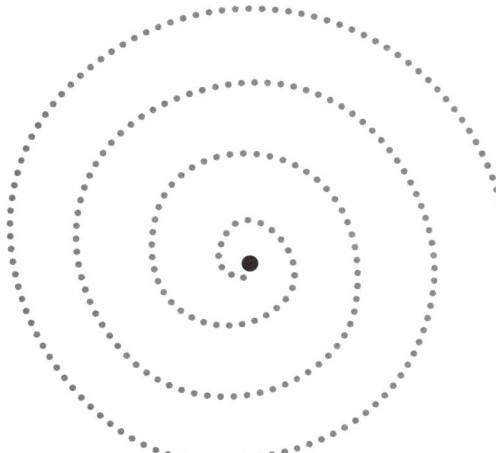

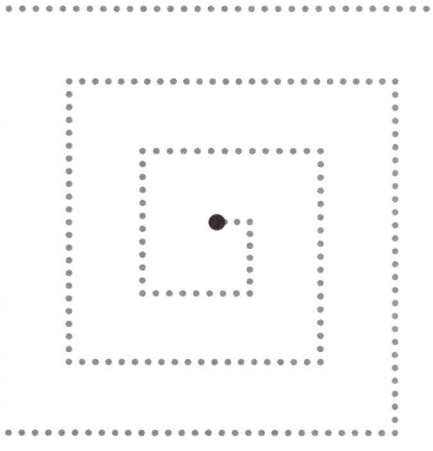

 Trace the firework patterns with bright colours.

 Join the dots to make the shape.

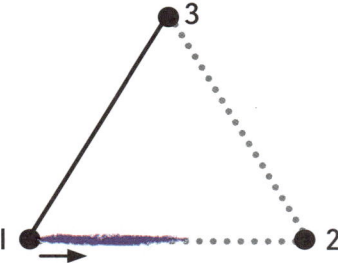

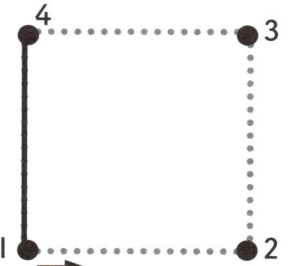

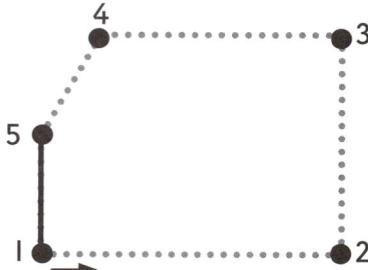

Trace the lines.

Whose shoes are these?

Trace this picture.

Well done!

Give yourself a sticker

Now – track how you're doing on page 32!

Going round (c, a and o)

 Trace the letters.

All these letters start at the top and go round.

The little flick at the end of the **a** will help you to join letters later on.

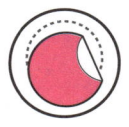 Find the things that start with **c**, **a** and **o**. Put the letter stickers in the right boxes.

 Trace the letters.

 Write three more letters at the end.

Remember to start at the top!

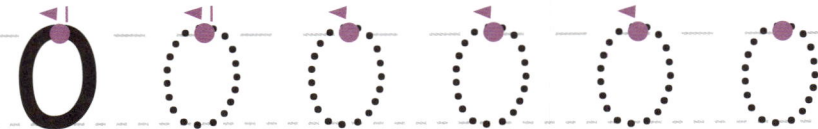

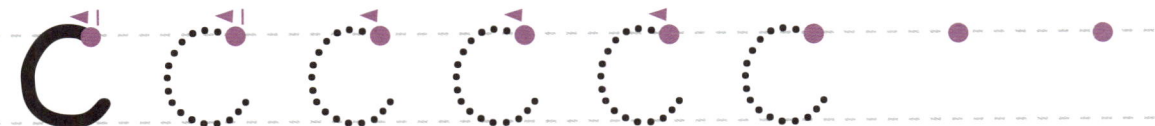

 Play with letters.

Spread out some flour on a wooden board. Write letters in the flour. Rub them out and try again.

Fill a resealable sandwich bag with hair gel (and perhaps a sprinkle of glitter). Flatten it down and make letter shapes in the gel.

Take a stick to the park. Find some muddy earth to draw letters in.

How else can you write the letters?

Give yourself a sticker

Now – track how you're doing on page 32!

Round and down (d, g and q)

Trace the letters.

All these letters start at the top and go all the way round.

Trace the letters.

Write three more letters at the end.

d d d d d d d • • •

g g g g g g g • • •

q q q q q q q • • •

 Find the letters that match.

 Trace each pair in a different colour.

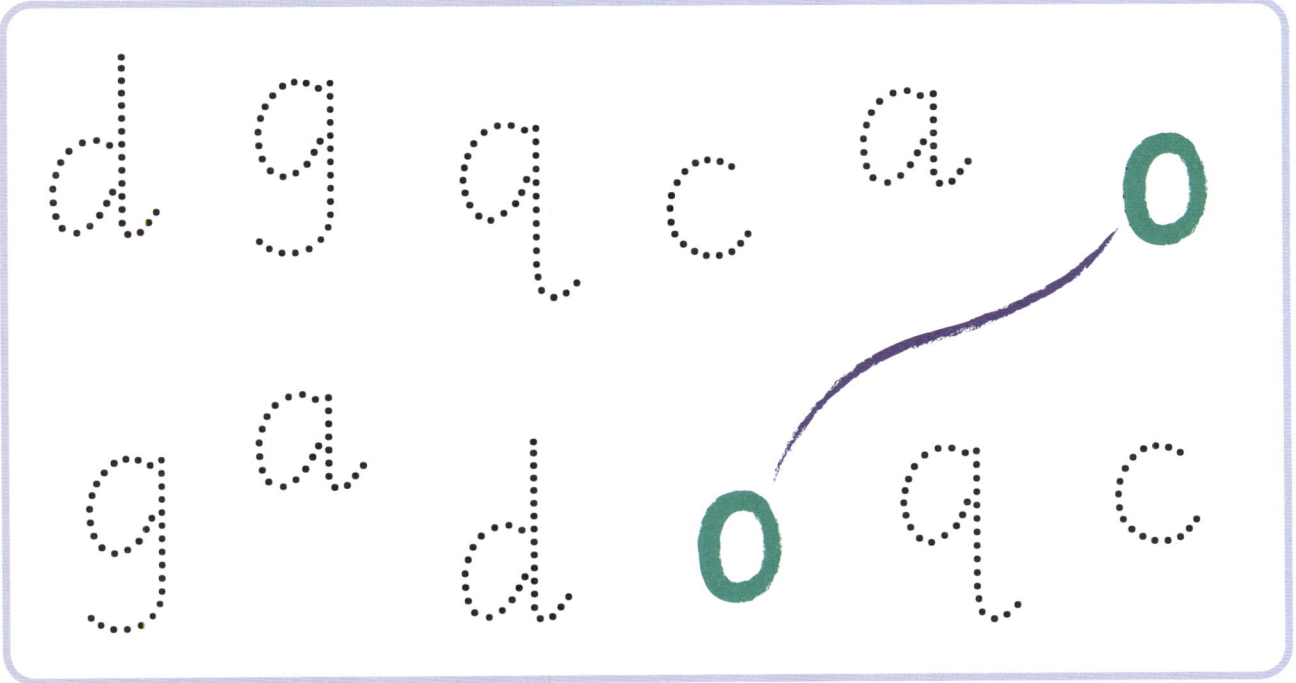

 Trace the words.

do   cog

add   go

dog

Well done!

Give yourself a sticker

Now – track how you're doing on page 32!

Round and round (e, f and s)

 Trace the letters.

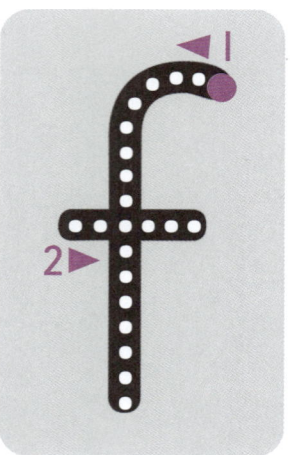

 ★★ Circle four of the same letters together.

I can see four of the letter c!

a	a	r	h	l	s	s	s	s	c
a	d	d	d	d	w	f	c	p	c
a	m	s	a	g	k	f	l	e	c
a	u	e	e	e	e	f	p	m	c
v	q	q	q	q	h	f	n	i	d
o	o	o	o	b	g	g	g	g	o

Trace the letters.

Write three more letters at the end.

Start in the middle. Go across, up, then around and down.

e e e e e e e . . . .

f f f f f f f . . . .

s s s s s s s . . . .

Trace the words.

Start at the top and go round.

fog fed
egg off so

Give yourself a sticker

Now – track how you're doing on page 32!

Dots and lines (i, l and t)

 Trace the letters.

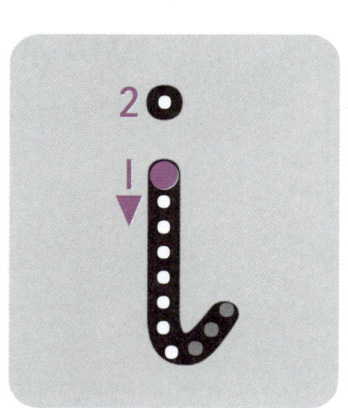 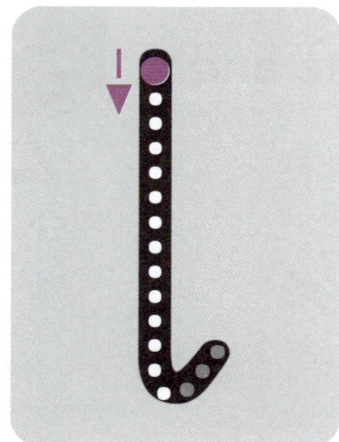 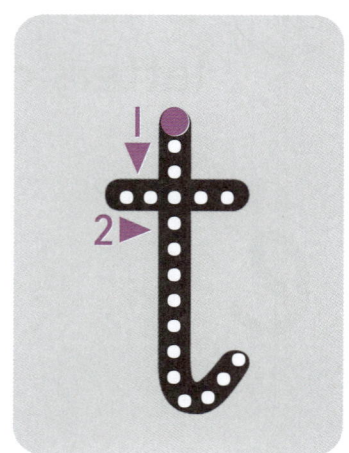

 Trace the letter **l** in these words.

log   lorry   ladder

 Trace the letter **t** in these words.

 tent    tap

 Trace the letter **i** in these words.

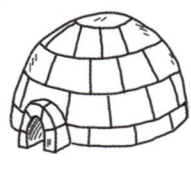 igloo    ice cream

 Trace the letters.

 Write three more letters at the end.

All these letters start at the top and go down.

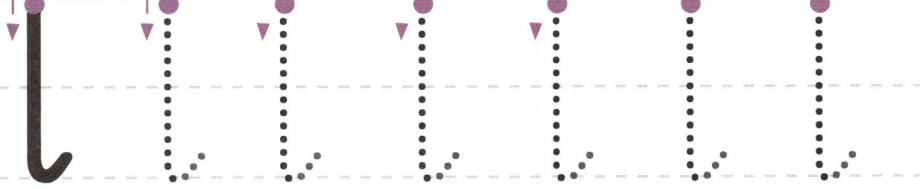

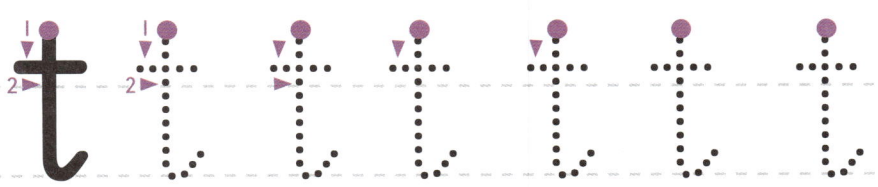

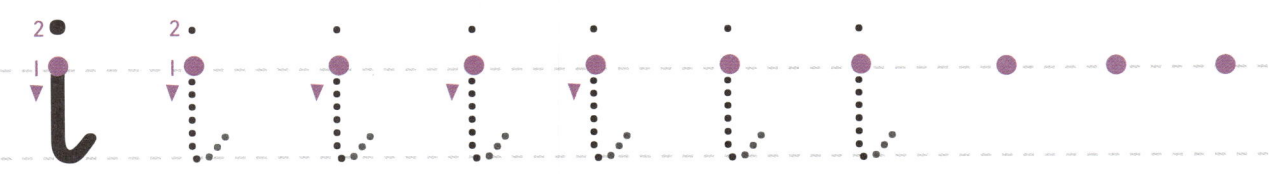

Don't forget the dot on the i!

 Play with letters.

Write a letter on a friend's back. Can they guess the letter?

Go for a walk. Can you see the letters i, l and t? Look at street signs and cars.

Give yourself a sticker

Now – track how you're doing on page 32!

Pencil grip check

 Hold your pencil.
Match it to the picture.

Are you still holding your pencil the right way?

Right hand

Left hand

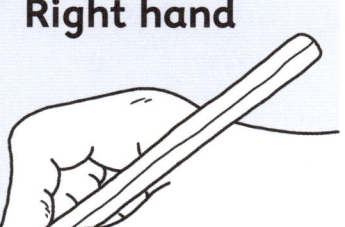

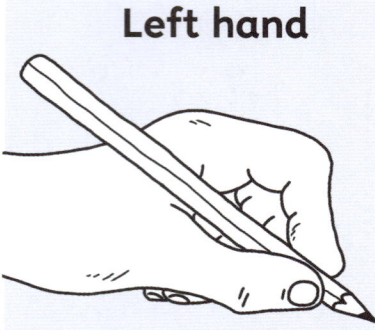

 Join the dots in the right order.

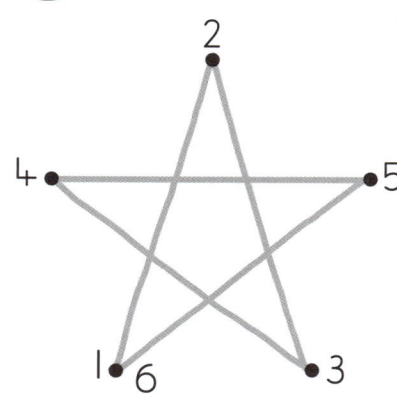

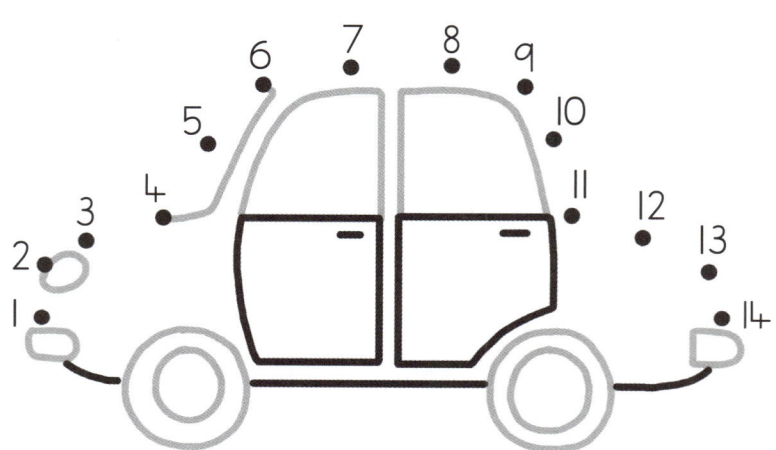

 Trace the patterns.

 Draw a path through the blocks to the other side.

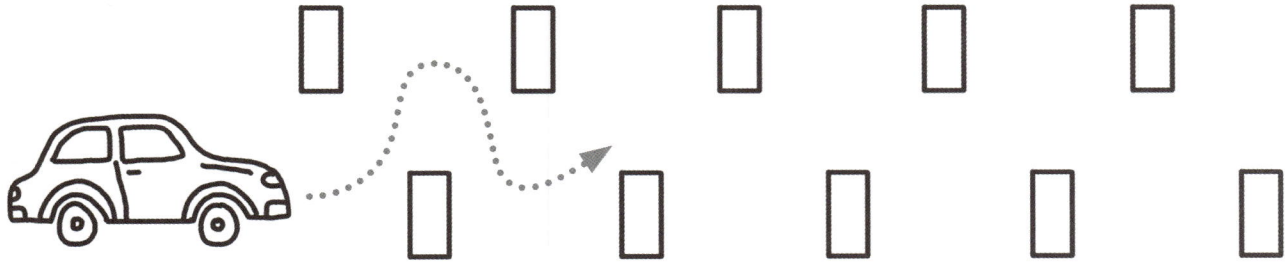

 Add eyes and smiles to these faces.

 Help Sill get out of the maze.

Give yourself a sticker

Now – track how you're doing on page 32!

Up and under (j, u and y)

 Trace the letters.

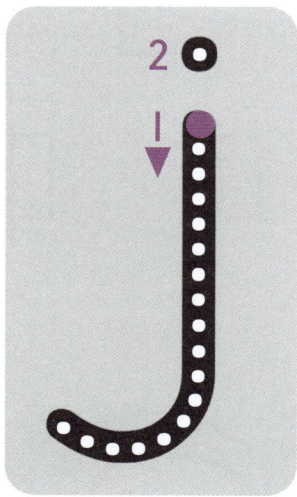

All these letters start at the top and go down and then round.

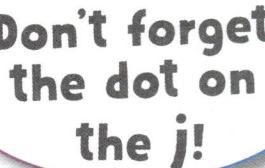 Trace the letters.

 Trace the letters.

 Write three more letters at the end.

Don't forget the dot on the j!

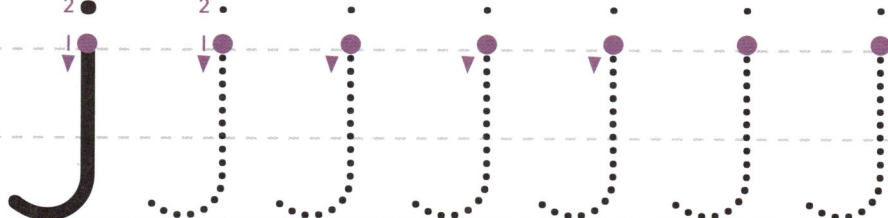

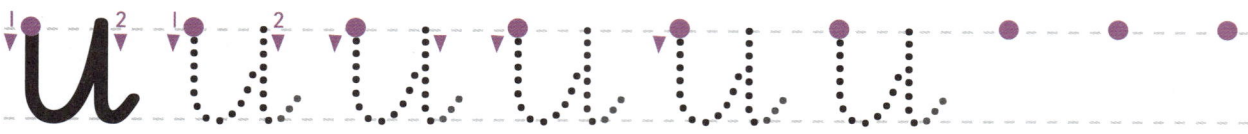

Stickers for page 6

a c

o

Stickers for page 17

s y d

g a o

t u f

Stickers for page 21

n n

n m

m m

n m

Character stickers

Reward Stickers

Well done! Well done!

Fantastic Work!

Great Job!

Well done! Well done!

Fantastic! Fantastic!

Well done! Well done!

Fantastic Work!

Great Job!

Well done! Well done!

Fantastic! Fantastic!

Well done! Well done!

Fantastic Work!

Great Job!

Well done! Well done!

Fantastic! Fantastic!

Trace the words.

Some letters have a tail that goes below the line.

yes   jet

jug   you   tug

Circle the letters that go below the line.

c g f a t j y u

o g e s y o q

Find the stickers that match the letters.

f   t   o

s   a   y

d   u   g

Give yourself a sticker

Now – track how you're doing on page 32!

Down, up and over (r and n)

 Trace the letters.

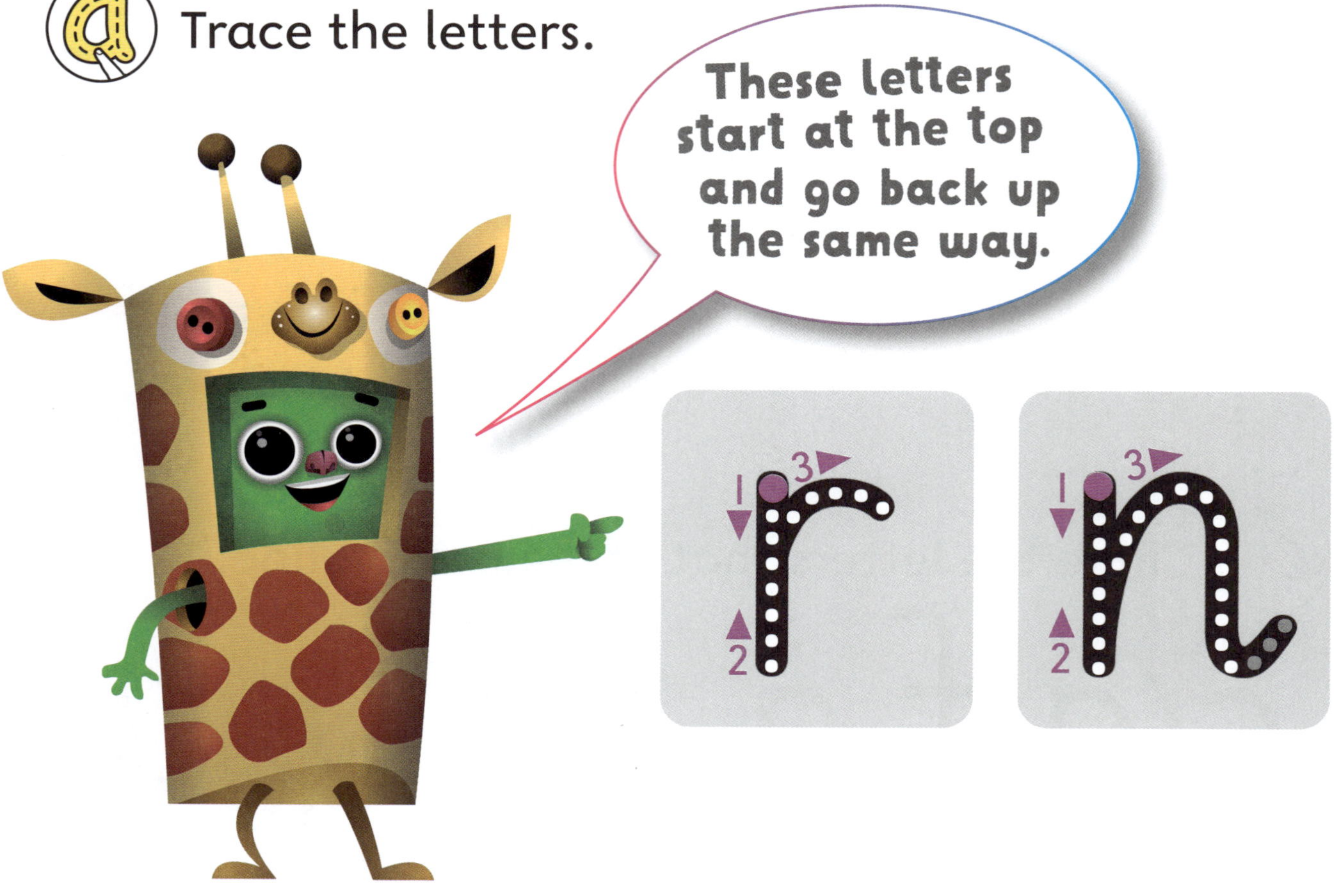

These letters start at the top and go back up the same way.

 Trace the letters.

Write three more letters at the end.

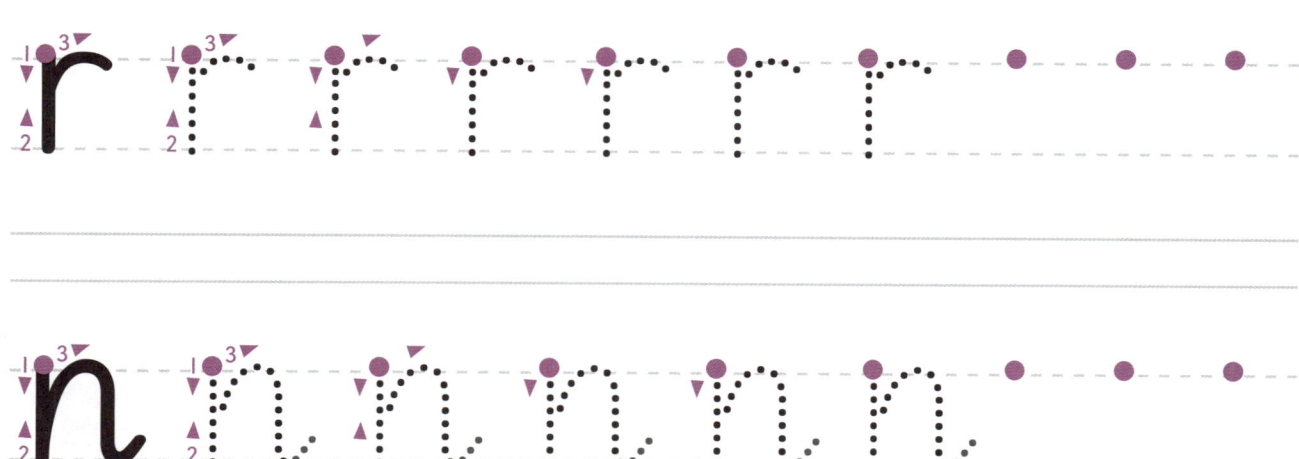

 Can you write these letters?

a [a] c [ ] n [ ]

g [ ] d [ ] o [ ]

f [ ] s [ ] e [ ]

r [ ]

 Play with letters.

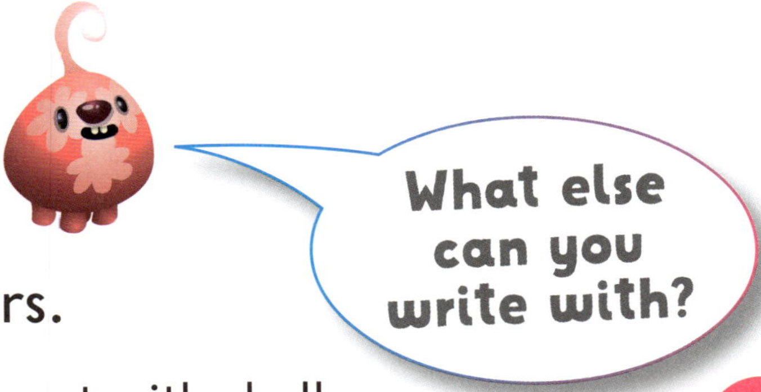

What else can you write with?

Write on the pavement with chalk.

Find a set of wooden or magnetic letters. Sort them into similar shapes. Think about the sound that they make.

Find objects around the house. What sound do they start with? Write the letter on a sticky note and stick it on the object. For example, put 't' on the television and 'd' on the door.

Give yourself a sticker

Now – track how you're doing on page 32!

More up and over (h and m)

 Trace the letters.

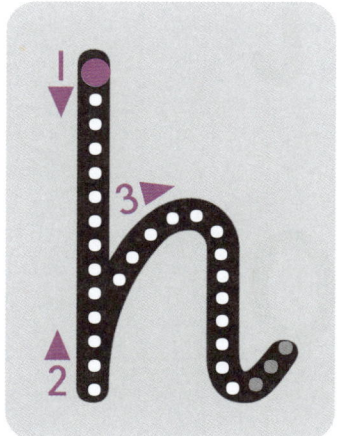

These letters start at the top and go back up the same way.

 Trace the pattern.

Trace the letters.

Write two more letters at the end.

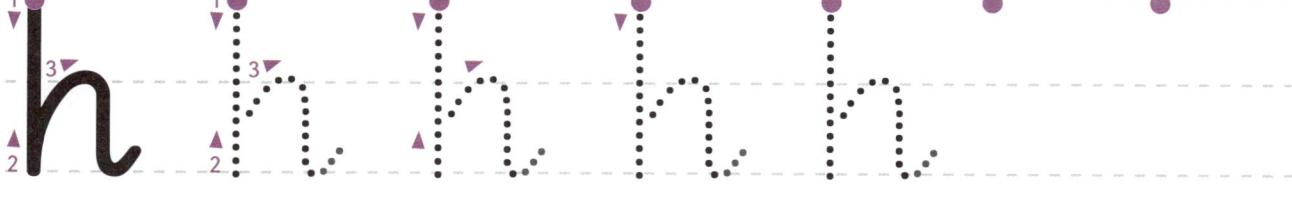

 Write the missing letters.
Use **m** or **h**.

Be careful – h only goes back up to halfway!

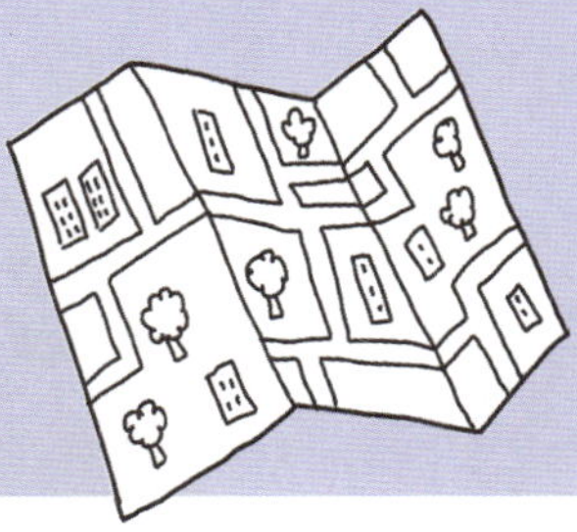

____at

Map

____oon

____oth

____ammer

____ut

 Match the stickers to the circles.

m

n

Give yourself a sticker

Now – track how you're doing on page 32!

Straight lines (b, k and p)

 Trace the letters.

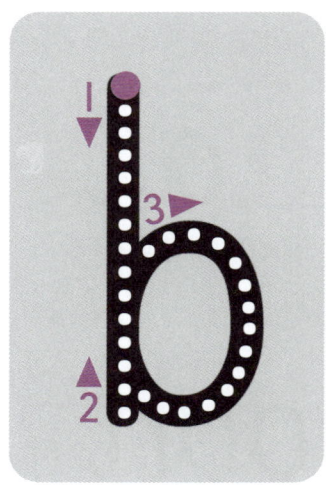
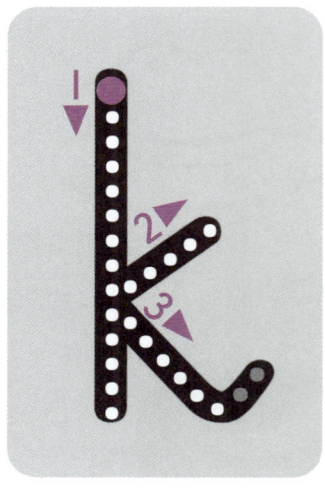

 Trace the letters.

 Write three more letters at the end.

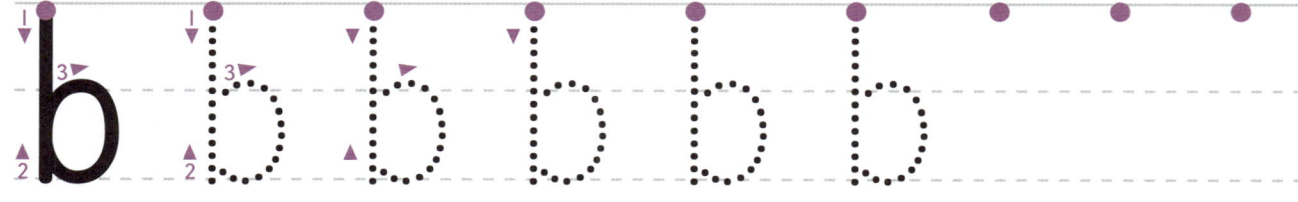

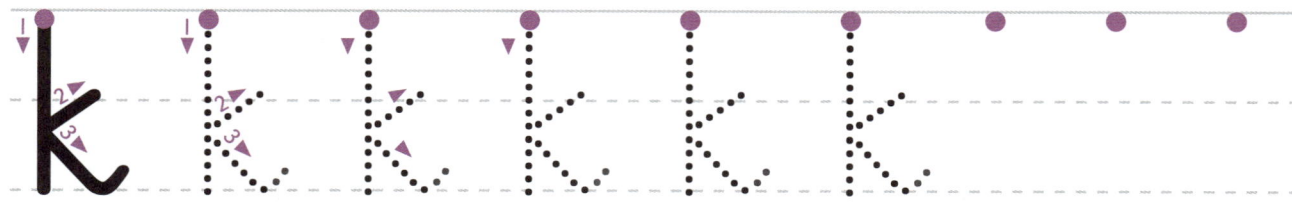

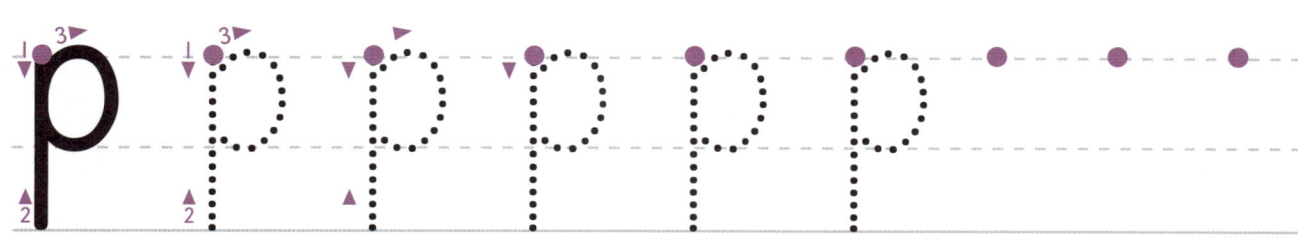

 **Write the letter that these objects begin with: b, k or p.**

b

p

k

Now – track how you're doing on page 32!

Give yourself a sticker

Crosses and zigzags (v, w, z and x)

 Trace the zigs and the zags.

 Match the letters to the fishing rods.

 Trace the letters.

Trace the letter **X**. Start at the top. Draw the first line. Take your pencil off the page. Start at the top again and draw the other line.

 Trace the letters.

 Write more letters at the end.

Give yourself a sticker

Now – track how you're doing on page 32!

Capital letters

 Trace the capital letters.

 Write the capital letters in the boxes.

Now can you write the capital letters yourself?

A A

B

C

D

E

F

G

H

I

J

K

L

Well done!

Give yourself a sticker

Now – track how you're doing on page 32!

All the letters

 Trace the letters.

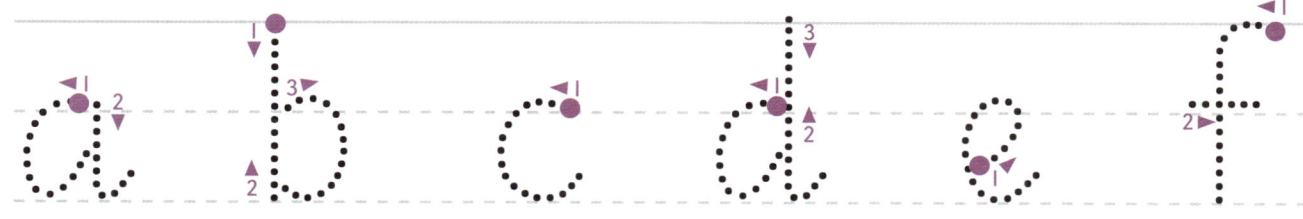

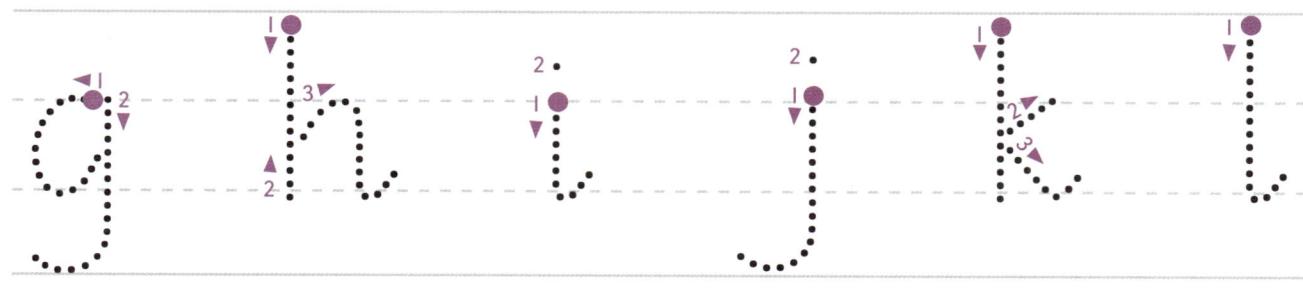

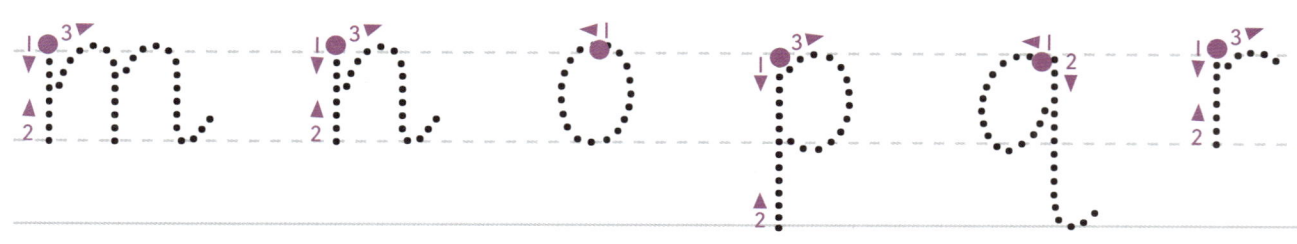

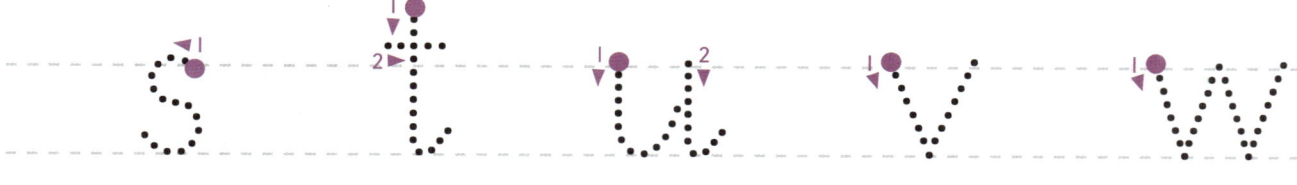

You did it! You can write the alphabet.

First words

 Trace the words.

 Write the word.

You can **write!**

the

to

I

onto

you

 Play with words.

Write a short sentence using some of the words on this page.

Read the words you have written.

Write a list of your favourite foods.

Give yourself a sticker

Now – track how you're doing on page 32!

More first words

Trace the word.

Write the word.

he

she

we

me

be

was

they

Read the words you have written.

no

go

all

are

 Write your name in the space.

can write!

 Play with words.

Make up a story using some of the words on pages 29, 30 and 31.

Write a label for your toys.

Try to write the names of your friends.

Give yourself a sticker

Now – track how you're doing on page 32!

Progress Chart

Colour in a face.

Page	I Can . . .	How did you do?
2–3	I can hold a pencil correctly.	☺ ☺ ☹
4–5	I can trace patterns.	☺ ☺ ☹
6–7	I can write c, a and o.	☺ ☺ ☹
8–9	I can write d, g and q.	☺ ☺ ☹
10–11	I can write e, f and s.	☺ ☺ ☹
12–13	I can write i, l and t.	☺ ☺ ☹
14–15	I can check my pencil grip.	☺ ☺ ☹
16–17	I can write j, u and y.	☺ ☺ ☹
18–19	I can write r and n.	☺ ☺ ☹
20–21	I can write h and m.	☺ ☺ ☹
22–23	I can write b, k and p.	☺ ☺ ☹
24–25	I can write v, w, z and x.	☺ ☺ ☹
26–27	I can write capital letters.	☺ ☺ ☹
28–29	I can write the alphabet.	☺ ☺ ☹
30–31	I can write some words.	☺ ☺ ☹

How did YOU do?